Scary Creatures
JELLYFISH

Written by
Gerard Cheshire

Created and designed
by David Salariya

FRANKLIN WATTS
An Imprint of Scholastic Inc.
NEW YORK • TORONTO • LONDON • AUCKLAND • SYDNEY
MEXICO CITY • NEW DELHI • HONG KONG
DANBURY, CONNECTICUT

Author:

Gerard Cheshire has written many books on natural history, and over the past twelve years has cultivated an excellent reputation as an author and editor. He now lives in Bath, England, with his wife and three sons.

Artists:

John Francis
Robert Morton
Carolyn Scrace

Series Creator:

David Salariya was born in Dundee, Scotland. In 1989 he established The Salariya Book Company. He has illustrated a wide range of books and has created many new series for publishers in the U.K. and overseas. He lives in Brighton, England, with his wife, illustrator Shirley Willis, and their son.

Editor: Stephen Haynes

Editorial Assistants:
Rob Walker, Tanya Kant

Picture Research:
Mark Bergin, Carolyn Franklin

Photo Credits:

Cadmium: 5
Nicolò Caneparo/Fotolia: 12
corsicarobase/Fotolia: 19
Mark Johnson/Fotolia: 8
Mountain High Maps/© 1993 Digital
    Wisdom Inc.: 20–21
Peter Parks/NHPA: 16
Linda Pitkin/NHPA: 7
Erika Walsh/Fotolia: 24
Wollwerth Imagery/Fotolia: 25

© The Salariya Book Company Ltd MMVIII
All rights reserved. No part of this book may be reproduced, stored in a retrieval system or transmitted in any form or by any means, electronic, mechanical, photocopying, recording or otherwise, without the written permission of the copyright owner.

Created, designed, and produced by
The Salariya Book Company Ltd
Book House
25 Marlborough Place
Brighton BN1 1UB

A CIP catalog record for this title is available from the Library of Congress.

ISBN-13: 978-0-531-20446-7 (Lib. Bdg.)
        978-0-531-21005-5 (Pbk.)
ISBN-10: 0-531-20446-4 (Lib. Bdg.)
        0-531-21005-7 (Pbk.)

Published in the United States by Franklin Watts
An Imprint of Scholastic Inc.
557 Broadway
New York, NY 10012

Printed in China

PAPER FROM
SUSTAINABLE
FORESTS

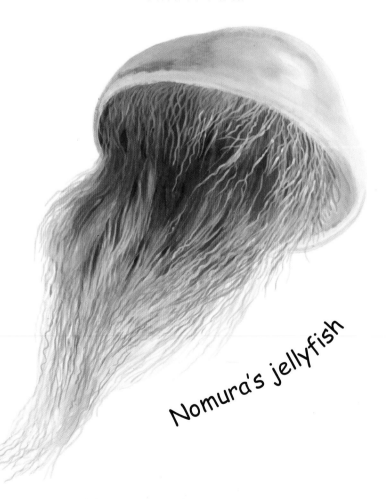

Nomura's jellyfish

Contents

Sea nettle

What Are Jellyfish?

Jellyfish belong to a group of animals that scientists call **cnidarians**, which includes corals and sea anemones. Although jellyfish look quite different from these other animals, they actually share the same very simple body design. They have a cup-shaped body with a single opening that is surrounded by tentacles. As their name suggests, they look sort of like jelly—but they don't look much like fish.

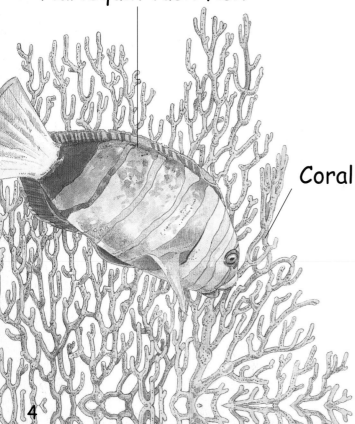

Harlequin tusk fish

Coral

Squid

Are squids related to jellyfish?

Although squids have jelly-like bodies and tentacles, they are not related to jellyfish. They have eyes and brains and belong to a more complex group of animals called **mollusks**.

Are corals related to jellyfish?

Corals are related to jellyfish, though they spend their lives in one place on the seabed instead of swimming about freely in the ocean. The tiny animals that make up the rock-like coral growths are called **polyps**.

Mauve stinger

Did You Know?

The jelly-like substance that makes up the outside of a jellyfish is called **mesoglea** or **ectoplasm**.

What Are Invertebrates?

The word **invertebrates** is used to describe all animals that do not have backbones. Backbones are made from bones called vertebrae, so animals with backbones are known as **vertebrates**, while those without are invertebrates. Jellyfish have a circular, or **radial,** design, with a network of nerves spreading out like the spokes of a wheel. They do not have a central nervous system, unlike a vertebrate, which has a brain and spinal column.

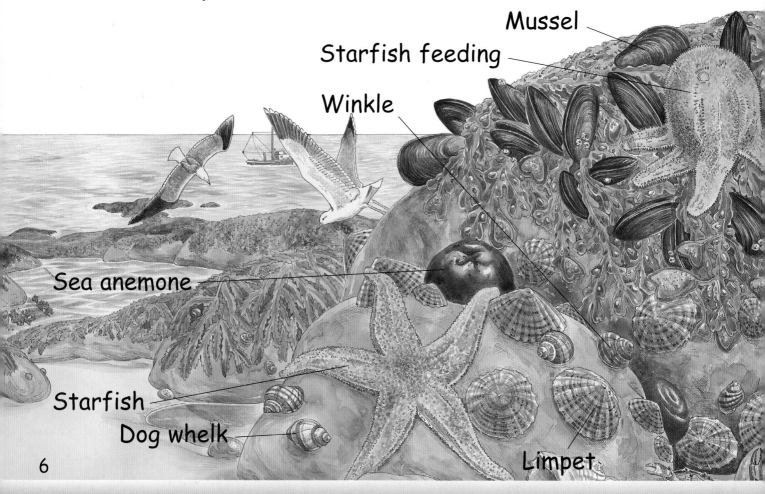

Mussel

Starfish feeding

Winkle

Sea anemone

Starfish

Dog whelk

Limpet

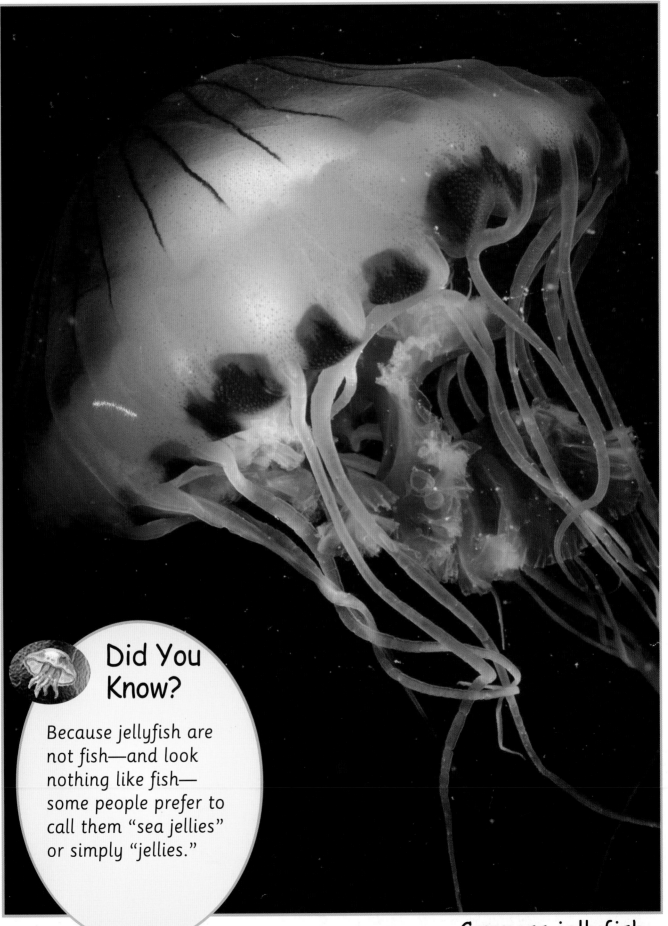

Did You Know?

Because jellyfish are not fish—and look nothing like fish—some people prefer to call them "sea jellies" or simply "jellies."

Compass jellyfish

How Do Jellyfish Reproduce?

Jellyfish have a complicated life cycle, with several different stages of development. Adult jellyfish are known scientifically as **medusas**. Their eggs hatch into **larvae** called **planulae** that drift about in the ocean until they settle on the surfaces of rocks. The planulae then attach themselves and grow into flower-like structures called polyps, similar to coral polyps. The polyp grows into a cone-like body called a **strobila**, which is like a stack of baby jellyfish. These babies, or **ephyrae,** swim off and gradually develop into full-sized medusas.

Did You Know?

Corals and sea anemones are familiar to us in their polyp stage, but jellyfish are usually seen in their medusa stage.

Sea nettles

The sea nettle is a type of jellyfish commonly found in coastal waters.

8

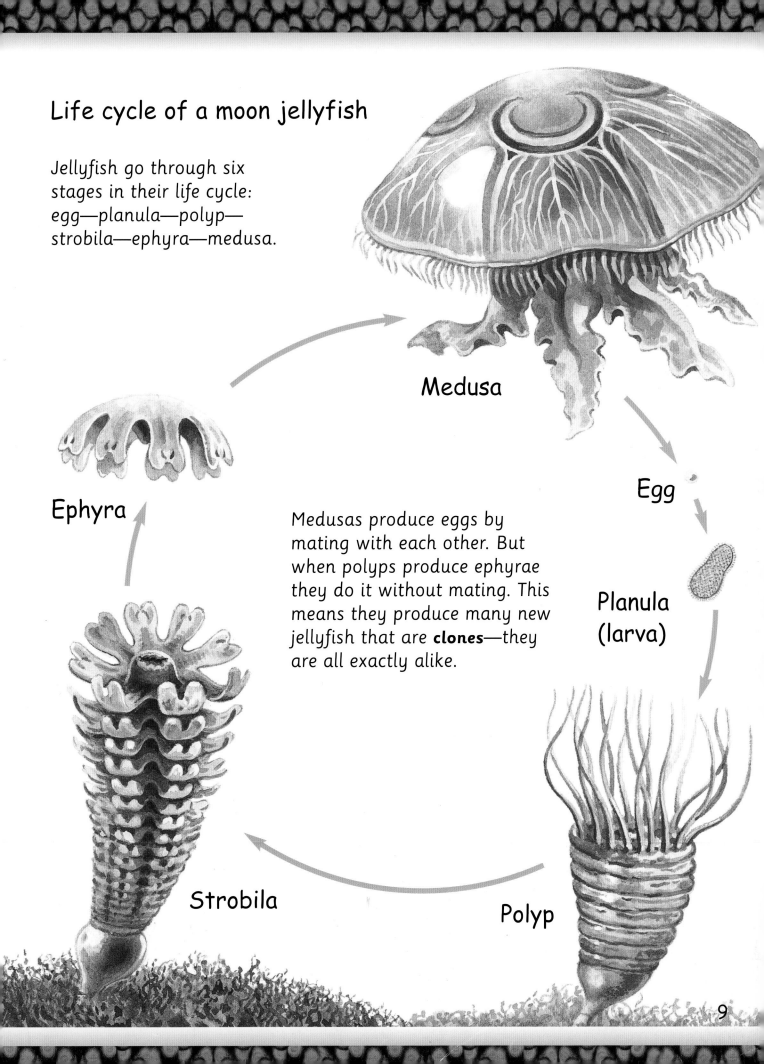

Life cycle of a moon jellyfish

Jellyfish go through six stages in their life cycle: egg—planula—polyp—strobila—ephyra—medusa.

Medusa

Ephyra

Medusas produce eggs by mating with each other. But when polyps produce ephyrae they do it without mating. This means they produce many new jellyfish that are **clones**—they are all exactly alike.

Egg

Planula (larva)

Strobila

Polyp

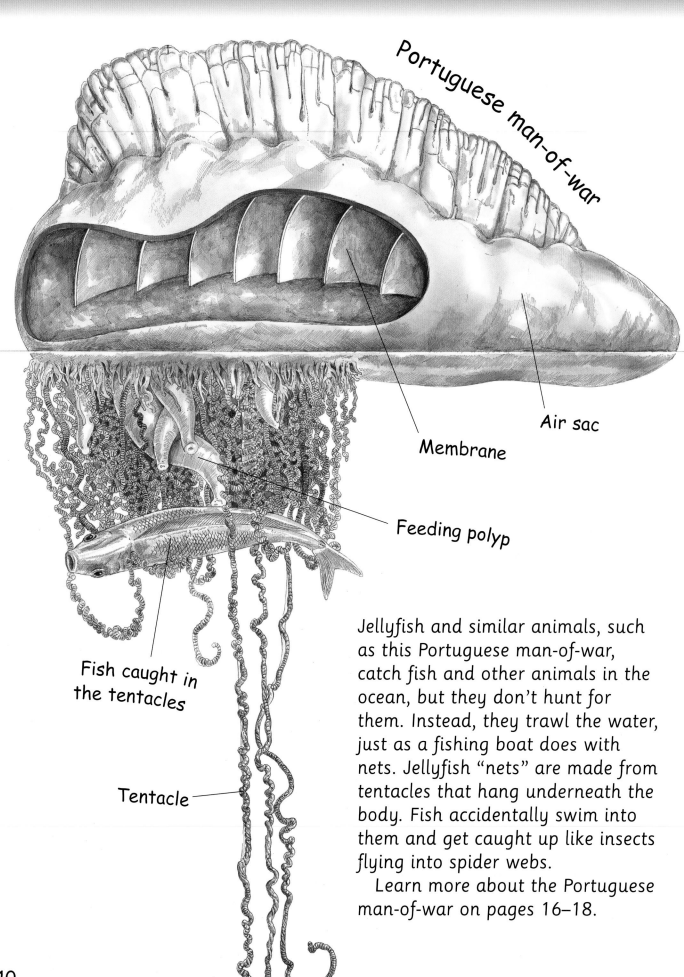

Air sac

Membrane

Feeding polyp

Fish caught in the tentacles

Tentacle

Jellyfish and similar animals, such as this Portuguese man-of-war, catch fish and other animals in the ocean, but they don't hunt for them. Instead, they trawl the water, just as a fishing boat does with nets. Jellyfish "nets" are made from tentacles that hang underneath the body. Fish accidentally swim into them and get caught up like insects flying into spider webs.

Learn more about the Portuguese man-of-war on pages 16–18.

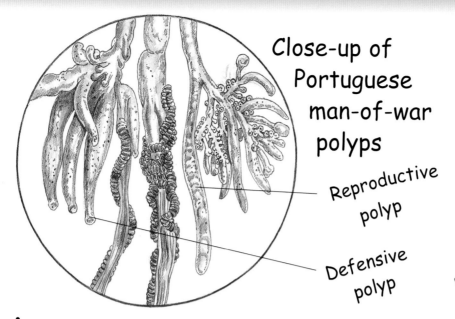

Close-up of Portuguese man-of-war polyps

Reproductive polyp

Defensive polyp

The diagrams below show what a nematocyst looks like through a microscope. When prey touches the stinging cell, the lid bursts off (middle picture) and the long, thin tube shoots out into the prey's body (top picture). The tube delivers the poison that paralyzes the prey. The barbs hook into the prey so it cannot escape.

How Do Jellyfish Feed?

When fish swim into the tentacles of a jellyfish, they get caught up and killed. The tentacles are covered with tiny stinging cells called **nematocysts**. When a fish rubs against them, the cells explode and fire microscopic darts into the skin of the fish. The darts are barbed so that they don't fall out, and they are armed with poisons, or **toxins**. The fish become paralyzed and die because they can't breathe. The tentacles then pass the dead fish to the mouth opening, so that the jellyfish can consume and digest its food.

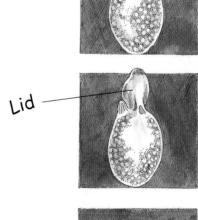

Barb

Tube

Lid

Cutaway view of the nematocyst

What's Inside a Jellyfish?

Jellyfish are very simple animals. A jellyfish is little more than a stomach surrounded by a bell-shaped body. Around the mouth opening hang many tentacles. There is only one entrance to the stomach, so jellyfish have to spit out their waste when they have finished digesting their food.

X-Ray Vision

Hold the next page up to the light and see what's inside a jellyfish.

See what's inside

Barrel jellyfish

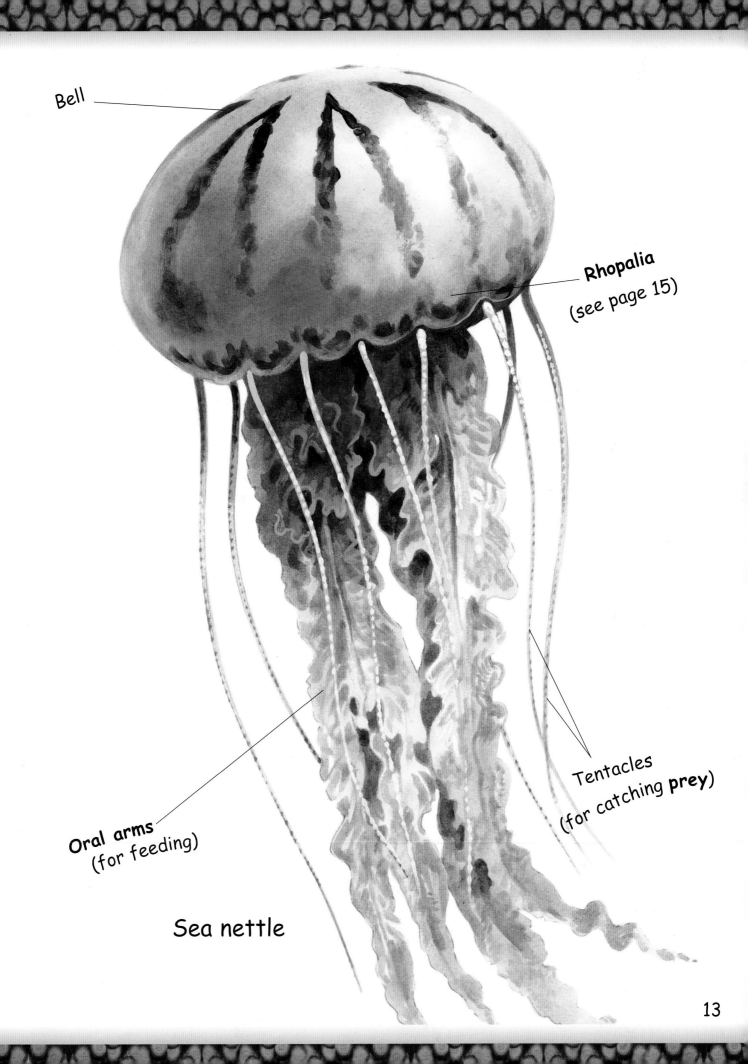

Bell

Rhopalia
(see page 15)

Oral arms
(for feeding)

Tentacles
(for catching **prey**)

Sea nettle

13

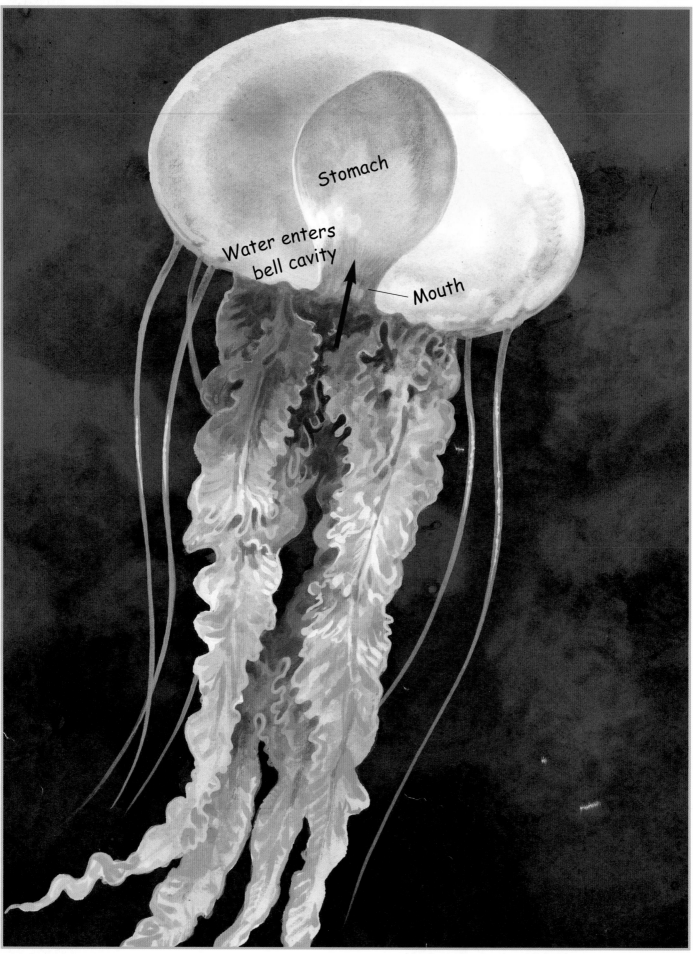

How Do Jellyfish Move?

Most jellyfish wander the oceans, letting the tides and currents move them around. They can move themselves up or down in the water when necessary. This helps them to find the best currents, to find mates, and to find food. They propel themselves by flexing their bell-shaped bodies and squeezing out water behind them.

Because jellyfish are made from jelly-like material, it is often possible to look through them and see the inside.

Did You Know?

Light-sensitive cells called rhopalia allow the jellyfish to know whether it is night or day. They also help in knowing which way is up and which is down, since it is light above and dark below. To avoid being eaten by turtles, jellyfish dive to deeper water during the day and come up to feed at night when the turtles cannot see them.

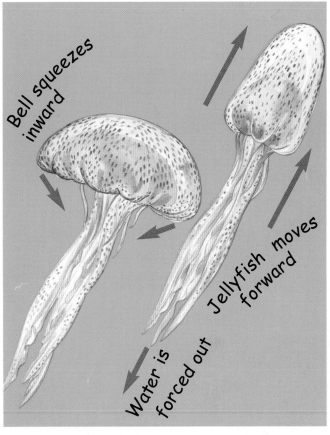

Bell squeezes inward

Jellyfish moves forward

Water is forced out

Muscles contract the edge of the bell so that it forces water backward and pushes the jellyfish forward. The bell is then allowed to open again, ready for the next stroke.

When Is a Jellyfish Not a Jellyfish?

Some animals look like jellyfish but aren't. The Portuguese man-of-war, which is related to the jellyfish, is a very unusual animal. In fact, it is actually a colony of animals joined together to help one another.

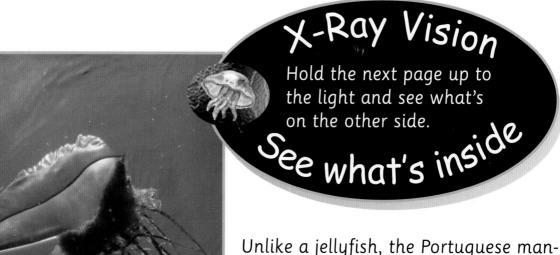

X-Ray Vision

Hold the next page up to the light and see what's on the other side.

See what's inside

Unlike a jellyfish, the Portuguese man-of-war floats on the surface of the water. It can't propel itself; wind and currents push it along. Each man-of-war is made up of four different types of animals: the balloon-like float and three kinds of polyps. One kind of polyp has tentacles that sting and capture prey. The second kind digests prey. And the third helps the colony reproduce. These creatures have a **symbiotic** relationship—they depend on each other to survive.

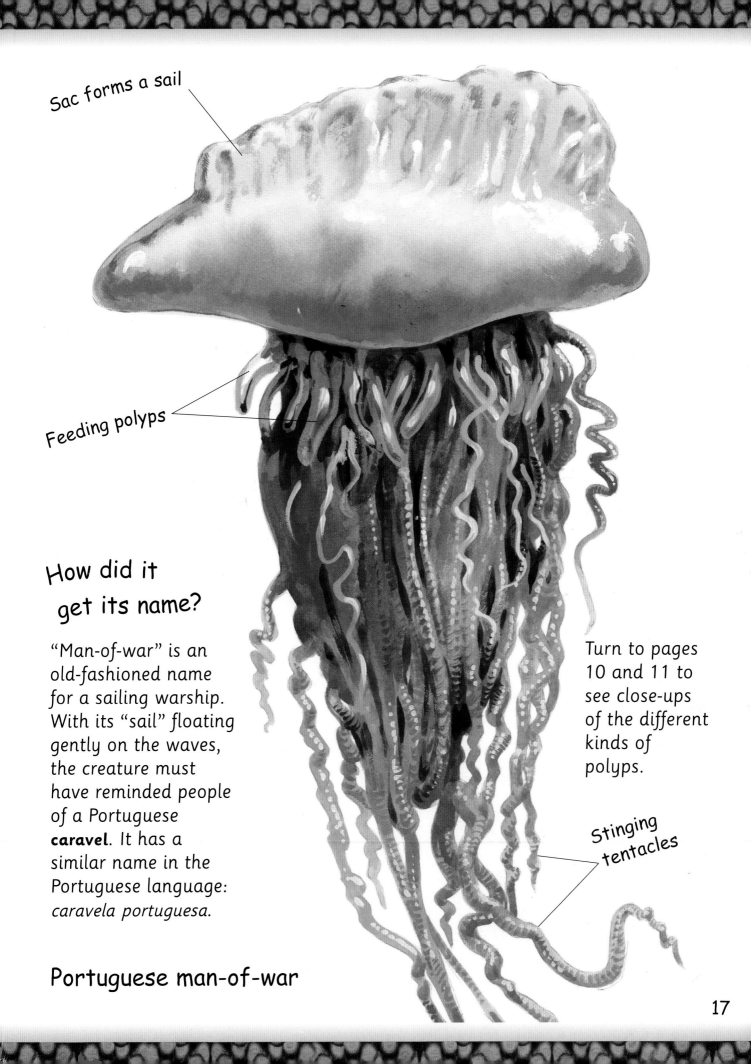

Sac forms a sail

Feeding polyps

How did it get its name?

"Man-of-war" is an old-fashioned name for a sailing warship. With its "sail" floating gently on the waves, the creature must have reminded people of a Portuguese **caravel**. It has a similar name in the Portuguese language: *caravela portuguesa*.

Turn to pages 10 and 11 to see close-ups of the different kinds of polyps.

Stinging tentacles

Portuguese man-of-war

Is It an Animal? Is It a Plant?

All animals need food. Some jellyfish—called Cassiopea or upside-down jellyfish—get around the problem of finding food by growing it themselves. Inside their see-through bodies they grow lots of very small plants called algae. The algae make food for the jellyfish from sunlight, using the process called photosynthesis.

These jellyfish sometimes look green because the algae contain chlorophyll, the chemical that makes photosynthesis possible. They live upside down, with their tentacles pointing upward like the branches of a tree. They look a little bit like ferns, because the tentacles are feathery in appearance so that the algae get as much sunlight as possible. The plants feed the jellyfish and the jellyfish protect the plants —another example of a symbiotic relationship.

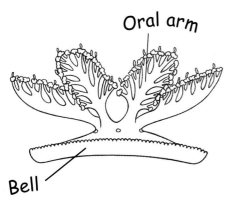

Oral arm

Bell

Diagram of Cassiopea

Upside-down jellyfish don't have stinging tentacles like other jellyfish. Thanks to their special relationship with the algae, they don't need to catch animals for food.

Upside-down jellyfish

19

Where Do Jellyfish Live?

Jellyfish of many different shapes and sizes live in the oceans of the world. They are successful because they reproduce in great numbers and feed on a wide variety of foods.

Lion's-mane jellyfish

This is the largest known jellyfish. It can be almost 8 feet (2.5m) wide and have tentacles that are 120 feet (37 m) long. It usually lives in the cold, deep waters of the Northern and Southern hemispheres.

North America

Pacific Ocean

South America

Sea nettle

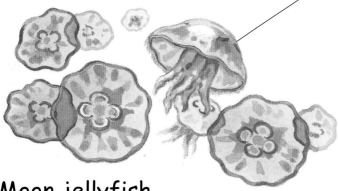

Moon jellyfish

One of the most common species, the moon jellyfish is about the size of a large dinner plate. It is often seen washed up on beaches, looking like a plate of jelly on the sand.

Portuguese man-of-war

This remarkable relative of the jellyfish is found in many parts of the world. It is often seen off the coast of Portugal.

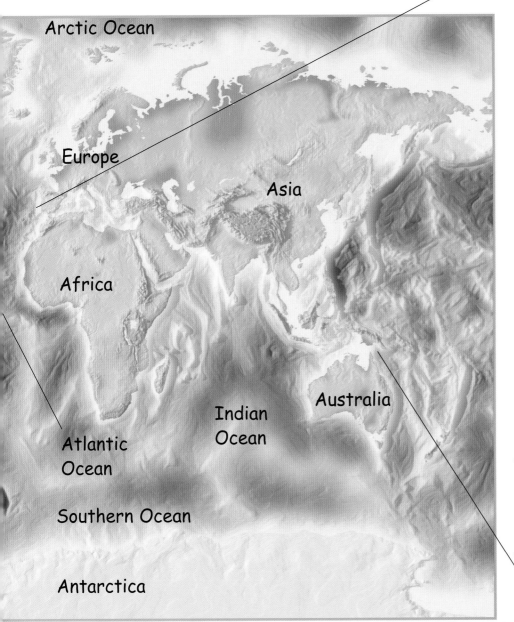

Arctic Ocean

Europe

Asia

Africa

Australia

Indian Ocean

Atlantic Ocean

Southern Ocean

Antarctica

Box jellyfish are the most dangerous to humans. They have box-shaped bells and very painful stings that feel like an attack by a swarm of wasps. Like the Portuguese man-of-war, they are not true jellyfish.

As their name suggests, sea nettles can give painful stings similar to those of a stinging nettle. The animals vary in color but are usually brownish with whitish spots.

Box jellyfish or sea wasp

What's the Largest Jellyfish?

The largest in the world is the lion's-mane jellyfish, which can grow to be as big as a small car, with a dome 8 feet (2.5 m) across. A jellyfish of similar size is Nomura's jellyfish. Both types can sting people, but they are usually far out to sea where people are not likely to swim. Their stings are not very strong; they use them only to catch small fish and other marine animals.

Did You Know?

Jellyfish have no skeleton to support their body. They collapse into a pile of jelly when they are removed from water, because the water helps them hold their shape.

One of the smallest jellyfish is the Irukandji jellyfish, which is only ½ inch by 1 inch (12 by 25 mm)—that's about the size of a small acorn. It has long tentacles that are hard to see and can give a very powerful sting. This sting doesn't hurt at first, but it paralyzes muscles, so people can drown from the effects.

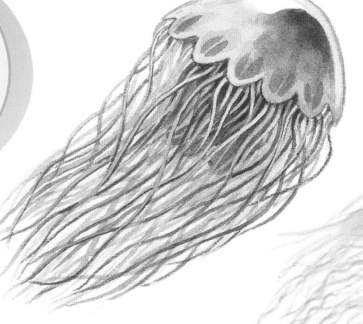

Lion's-mane jellyfish
Up to 8 feet (2.5m) wide

When naturalists swim alongside large jellyfish to study and film them, they have to wear protective clothing so that they don't get stung by the tentacles. Really big jellies are capable of catching large fish, but they usually catch lots of small ones instead.

Nomura's jellyfish
Up to 8 feet
(2.5m) wide

Average-sized jellyfish

Most jellyfish are fairly small. This means they don't need so much food to survive, but it also means they are more likely to be eaten by **predators** themselves.

How Long Do Jellyfish Live?

Most jellyfish complete their life cycle in a year. They follow the changing seasons and become adults when the oceans are at their calmest and warmest. When the oceans are cold and stormy, the jellyfish are safely stuck to rocks in the polyp stage of their life.

One type of jellyfish is said to be immortal, which means that it lives forever. It can return to its polyp stage after it has been an adult or medusa. Can it keep changing back and forth for as long as it likes? Scientists are not sure.

Moon jellyfish

The moon jellyfish is easy for scientists to study, because it is not too big and its sting is not powerful enough to pierce human skin.

Is this a jellyfish?

Comb jellies or Ctenophora* are not really jellyfish, but they are related to jellyfish. Like jellyfish, they have jelly-like bodies with a circular or radial design, but they have no stinging cells. There are about a hundred species of comb jellies. The largest are up to 5 feet (1.5m) in diameter, but most are very small—about an inch (2.5 cm) across. Most comb jellies are transparent—which makes it very difficult for their prey to see them—but some deep-sea species are brightly colored.

* pronounced "ten-o-for-a" or "teen-o-for-a"

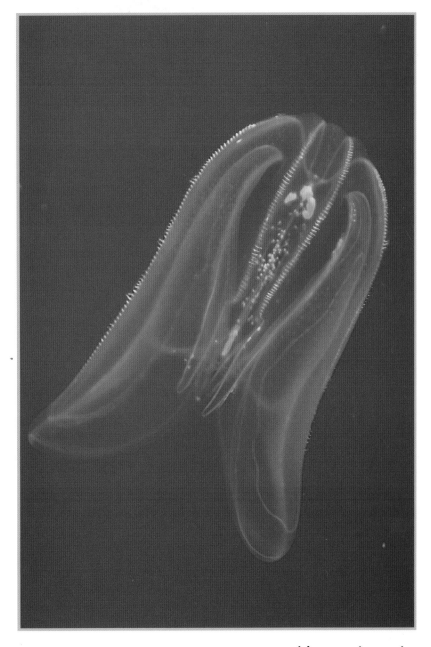

Mnemiopsis

Did You Know?

Some jellyfish, and some comb jellies, can produce light by a process called **bioluminescence**, just like glowworms and fireflies. This enables them to communicate in the dark—either at night or deep beneath the sea.

This small comb jelly may not look scary, but it has caused a lot of damage in some parts of the world. It eats so many fish eggs and other small animals that larger predators do not have enough to eat.

Are Jellyfish Dangerous?

They can be! Most jellyfish have tentacles covered with stinging cells or nematocysts (see page 11). They sting their prey to paralyze them and keep them from escaping. When they sting humans, the sting is usually quite mild, but some types of jellyfish are quite dangerous. If people get stung in shallow water, they can usually get out safely. But there is always a risk of drowning when swimmers are stung in deep water; the stings can be so painful that the victim cannot swim.

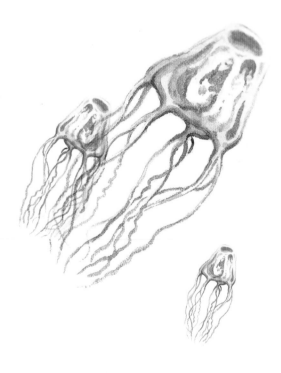

Box jellyfish

The box jellyfish or sea wasp is the most dangerous to humans. It has long tentacles that can wrap around people's bodies, covering them in nasty wounds. Victims often receive more stings as they try to get away.

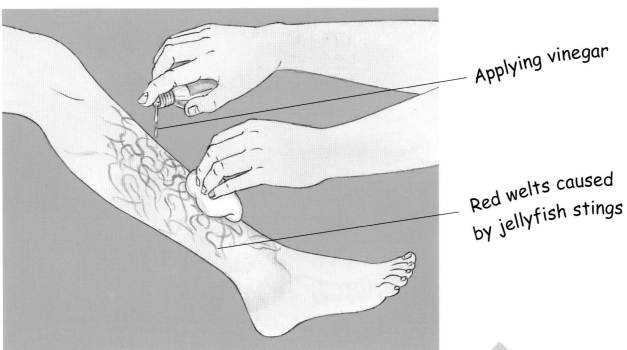

Applying vinegar

Red welts caused by jellyfish stings

What if you do get stung?

Vinegar is the key to treating jellyfish stings when they first happen. The acid in the vinegar neutralizes the toxin and stops the sting from getting worse. Vinegar also stops any sting cells left on the skin from stinging. Once at the hospital, patients can be treated with antivenom.

Jellyfish warning sign

 ## Did You Know?

Wearing pantyhose or tights made of nylon fabric prevents box jellyfish from stinging. The thin layer of fabric is enough to keep the tentacles from touching your skin.

What Eats Jellyfish?

In their adult stage, as medusas, jellyfish are pretty good at defending themselves from being eaten by predators. During other stages of development they are eaten by all kinds of ocean creatures. This is why they reproduce in extremely high numbers, so that enough of them survive to the adult stage.

Several species of sea turtle eat mainly adult jellyfish. Their throats and stomachs have very thick walls to protect them from stings.

When jellyfish are in their planula and ephyra stages they are **zooplankton** (small drifting creatures), along with the larvae of many other animals. Zooplankton are eaten by fish, squid, krill, and filter-feeding giants such as sharks and whales.

 ## Did You Know?

Sea turtles often mistake plastic bags for jellyfish. When they eat them they can't digest the bags or spit them out, and they eventually choke or starve to death.

Jellyfish Facts

Jellyfish are animals, although some look more like plants.

They have more phases in their life cycle than other animals.

Jellyfish have no bones; they are invertebrates. They belong to the very primitive class of invertebrates known as *scyphozoans*. The word comes from "skyphos," which is Greek for "cup" and refers to the shape of the animal's body.

Jellyfish have no eyes, brains, or blood. They also don't have lungs or gills. They absorb oxygen through their skins instead.

Not all jellyfish have tentacles. The blubber jellyfish has oral arms, but no tentacles.

Jellyfish vary in size, from the size of a fingernail to the size of a small car.

Jellyfish are radially symmetrical—circular—in shape. Humans and other vertebrates are bilaterally symmetrical—they have two sides, and one is a mirror image of the other.

Jellyfish first appeared 650 million years ago, long before animals first walked on land. Humans appeared only about 4 million years ago.

Some jellyfish, like the cannonball jellyfish, are edible. They may be farmed in the future to provide protein.

Jellyfish can be kept as pets in an aquarium, but they are difficult to care for properly. Freshwater jellyfish are easier to keep than saltwater species.

Jellyfish can be found in deep-sea habitats. The erenna jellyfish has a lure that glows red in the dark to attract small fish, which it then eats.

Jellyfish are usually about 95% water, which means that only 5% is left when they dry out.

Some jellyfish species have been known to feed on other jellyfish.

There are thousands of species of jellyfish worldwide.

Jellyfish groups are known as "smacks" of jellyfish.

Jellyfish live in every ocean of the world.

Glossary

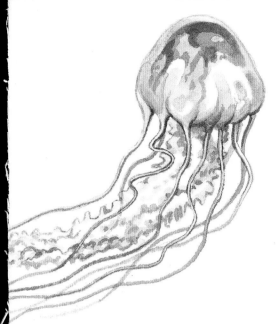

bioluminescence The ability that some animals have to glow in the dark.

caravel A small sailing ship of the 15th and 16th centuries.

clone An animal which grows from its parent without mating.

cnidarian The scientific name for jellyfish and related animals.

ectoplasm Another word for **mesoglea**.

ephyra (plural **ephyrae**) A young medusa.

invertebrate An animal with no backbone.

larva A young animal that will change into a different form when it becomes an adult.

medusa (plural **medusae** or **medusas**) The adult form of a jellyfish.

mesoglea The jelly-like substance that forms the outside layer of a jellyfish.

mollusks A group of invertebrates that includes snails, slugs, shellfish, octopuses, and squids.

nematocyst A stinging cell on a jellyfish tentacle.

oral arms The inner ring of tentacles around the mouth of a jellyfish.

planula The larva of a jellyfish, which floats freely in the sea.

polyp A cylinder-shaped, hollow animal with tentacles that may be connected to a colony of polyps; jellyfish go through a polyp stage.

predator An animal that kills other animals for food.

prey An animal that is killed and eaten by a predator.

radial Spreading outward like the spokes of a wheel.

rhopalium (plural **rhopalia**) A light-sensitive organ on the rim of a jellyfish's body.

strobila A jellyfish polyp which is about to produce **ephyrae**.

symbiotic A word describing living things that are dependent on one another for survival.

toxin A poison from a plant or an animal.

vertebrate An animal with a backbone.

zooplankton Small creatures that drift about in the sea, not swimming but moved by the current.

31

Index

AUG 2 9 2008